The Jack-O-Lantern

To everyone who
enjoys the fall season
and pumpkins!

I have 1 orange oval pumpkin.

I draw 2 triangles for the eyes.

I draw 1 circle for the nose.

I draw 1 rectangle for the mouth.

I ask 1 adult
to help me
to cut the
top.

We use 2 spoons to scoop the inside.

1...2...3...

We cut out 2 triangles for the eyes.

We cut 1 circle for the nose.

We cut 1 rectangle for the mouth.

Lastly,
We put 1 light
inside the
pumpkin.

Happy Halloween!

You turn!!!

Get a pumpkin and ask an adult to help, then make your very own Jack-O-lantern!!

Draw your own Jack-o-lantern design!

www.ingramcontent.com/pod-product-compliance
Lightning Source LLC
LaVergne TN
LVHW071228160826
845679LV00003B/933

* 9 7 8 1 7 3 8 7 9 9 5 4 1 *